The Rain Prince

Written by
Laura Napier

Illustrated by
Marea Claybourne-Napier

Story by
Laura Napier and Marea Claybourne-Napier

PAGE PUBLISHING
Conneaut Lake, PA

First originally published by Page Publishing 2021

Cover Design by Lauren Swintek
Illustrations by Marea Claybourne-Napier

ISBN 978-1-6624-6297-9 (pbk)
ISBN 978-1-6624-6344-0 (hc)
ISBN 978-1-6624-6298-6 (digital)

Printed in the United States of America

To Marea McKenzie Rose Claybourne-Napier in all her brilliance, creativity, and love which she has brought into our world.

And for all the other Brown Princesses in the world.

baby
rainbow

King Martin

Rainbows castle

Queen Angela

Once upon a time, in a land that is close by but far from the seeing eye, there lived a king, a queen, and a prince. The prince had been left on the castle doorstep as a baby by his birth mother. Although she loved him, she could not care for him, and so she had found one who could: the queen.

T he queen adopted the boy and named him Rainbow. Indeed, he was like a rainbow, for his skin changed color as often as his mood: green when he was uneasy, blue when he was sad, orange when he was afraid, red when he was angry, and a warm brown when he was happy.

Rainbow was a fine young man, and the people of the kingdom loved him. The kingdom's subjects all had different skin colors, and in their prince, they each saw a piece of themselves. There was only one who lived nearby who did not care for Rainbow—a man by the name of A. W. Ful.

A. W. Ful disliked anyone who looked different from him. Disgusted by the idea that a boy whose skin could change colors would someday rule the land, A. W. Ful decided to rid the kingdom of the prince.

He hired a White Wizard, who had skin as white as snow, to curse Rainbow. The Wizard cast Rainbow into a deep sleep to last forever.

White Wizard
A.W.ful Man and cast a spell or rainbow

With a potion from the Mother of the Forest, a magical wise woman, the queen's love revived the prince. The Mother of the Forest did warn the queen:

"**Y**our kiss cannot last forever. Love like 'Freedom must be earned and won every generation."[1] If he is not kissed by his true love by the time he is twenty-one, he will again fall into a deep sleep."

Mother of the forest's house

Mother of the forest

Silvia

---

[1] Coretta Scott King.

So it was that the boy grew and neared his twenty-first birthday with a curse hanging over his head...

One day, as Rainbow is playing with a group of schoolchildren, a beautiful young woman arrives being carried on a litter. Her name is Circa.

Circa arrives...

rainbow & circa drinking lemonade in gazebo

Seeing Circa, Rainbow is smitten. He invites her for lemonade, and she happily accepts. From that moment on, the two are rarely apart. Soon, Rainbow asks Circa to marry him, and she says yes. Rainbow is always greenish with Circa, but he knows not why.

Weeks later, Rainbow sees another new face in the kingdom. "Who is that?" he asks one of the schoolchildren. "That is our new teacher, Marea," the boy says. "Isn't she pretty?"

"Indeed," Rainbow says, intrigued.

Over the next days, Rainbow watches Marea. Finally, he introduces himself. As the two speak, he learns that they have much in common, including the desire to one day have many of their own rainbow-colored children.

Rainbow does not know that Marea is also a princess, though her parents died when she was young and her riches were stolen.

Baby Marea with her mom and dad the other King and Queen

Marea's castle

Rainbow loves how Marea works with the children and often comes to watch her teach. Rainbow is also confused. With Marea, his skin turns a deep shade of brown, and he feels an ease he never feels with Circa.

The queen and rainbow. Marea is behind them

One day, the queen spies Rainbow watching Marea. "She's wonderful, isn't she?" the queen whispers. Rainbow is quiet, but his skin turns a dark brown. "Perhaps she is the one," the queen says. "I've never seen you look so at Circa." Rainbow shakes his head. "I made a vow to Circa. I will keep my word."

At last, the day of Rainbow's wedding arrives.

Circa

Rainbow Wedding With circa

the wedding

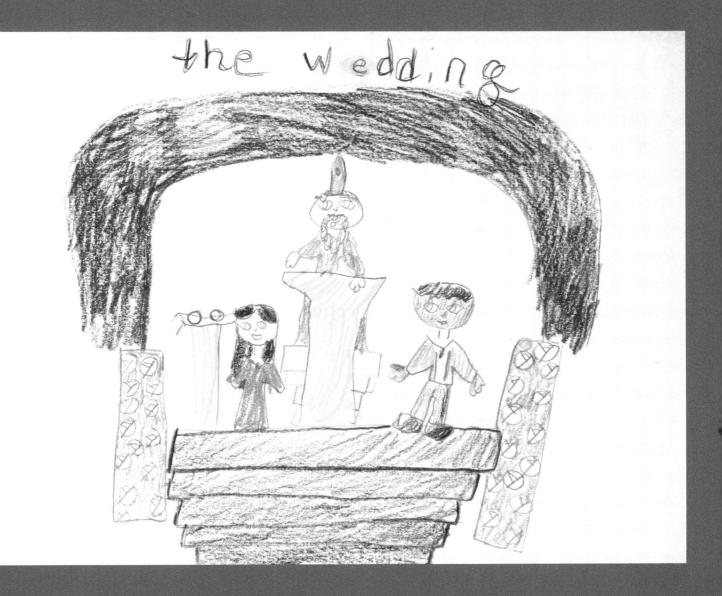

Marea is riding through the field when she hears an awful laugh.

Peering through bushes, Marea sees the White Wizard and A. W. Ful. "I can't wait to see the king's and queen's colorful faces drain to white when their precious prince falls into his forever sleep, and his wife cannot wake him because she does not love him!" A. W. Ful says.

Mare a hearing Aw.ful and keeky talking

A.W. ful + Keeky, laughing evilly

"What a marvelous idea it was to send Circa to marry him!" the White Wizard says.

M

area gasps, then races toward the kingdom...

the chase to the wedding

Meanwhile, in the castle garden, the wedding is underway...

Wedding

Queen at Wedding

Albert

"Do you, Circa, take Rainbow to be your partner in life?" asks the Justice of the Peace. "I do!" Circa smiles.

Circa at Wedding

Rainbow Wedding With circa

26

"Do you, Rainbow—"

"Stop!" Marea shouts as she rides up. "You can't marry her! She does not love you!" Rainbow looks up in surprise.

"Marea?"

"She was sent by A. W. Ful!" Marea shouts. "I heard him talking to the White Wizard! If you marry her, you will never find your true love!"

Rainbow faces Circa, his skin a pale green. "Is this true?"

The Awful Man and the White Wizard burst into the ceremony. "Is it done?" A. W. Ful asks. Circa shakes her head...

Marea arrives at the Prince's Wedding

Rainbow runs to Marea, his skin changing to brown. He climbs onto Marea's horse. The White Wizard points his wand at Rainbow and utters a spell. There is a flash of white light, and Rainbow falls asleep. "He must be kissed by another love!" the Mother of the Forest yells. The queen looks at Marea. "If you love him, kiss him. You have his mother's permission."

As Marea looks down at Rainbow, the White Wizard raises his wand. Raising her hand, the Mother of the Forest says, "Halt all evil from this place, and all bad will be set against its creator's face."

A.W.ful and keekky tied up by silvia

The White Wizard's wand spins, casting its spell on the Wizard and A. W. Ful, who fall to the ground, asleep.

With a soft smile, Marea bends over and kisses Rainbow's forehead. Rainbow's eyes flutter and open. "You love me?" he asks Marea, his skin turning deep brown. "From the beginning," says Marea. "Until the end of the rainbow?" Rainbow asks. Marea nods. "Forever. Past the sky."

"That's a long time," Rainbow says with a smile. "But not long enough with you."

What character did you like best in this book?

Why did you like this character best?

What was your favorite part of the book?

About the Authors

Laura Napier, also known as L. D. Napier, writes in many forms including screenplays, plays, essays, and novels. She has written several children's books dealing with race, identity, and brown princesses, inspired by her daughter.

Most recently Laura directed *The Rainbow Prince*, a thirty-minute short film based on this original book.

In 2008, Napier wrote, directed, and coproduced an off-Broadway play at La MaMa in New York City called *The G Word: For Those Born Later* as a fundraiser for schools and a women's center in Darfur. Laura has taught filmmaking at universities, including Temple, Loyola, and CUNY, playwriting to inner-city students, and film at the Solebury

School. Laura taught writing as an artist in residence at Soledad maximum-security prison in California to learn from inside.

Laura has received many awards, including a Mid-Atlantic Regional Media Arts Fellowship, a Telly award, and the International Health & Medical Media Award for her documentaries.

Laura's goal is to continue to echo the times with a loud voice in which George Bernard Shaw, Langston Hughes, Ann Petry, and James Baldwin would be proud.

Marea Claybourne-Napier likes to draw and to read. She writes her own books and plays. She likes to adapt plays, design costumes, and then put them on by her dolls. Marea plays the piano and the cello. She is ten years old.

www.therainbowprince.com

CPSIA information can be obtained
at www.ICGtesting.com
Printed in the USA
BVHW020204110322
631230BV00016B/733